Trading Book For Beginners

Your Step-By-Step Guide to Navigating the Financial Markets with Confidence.

Chinedu Brown

Copyright© 2024 Chinedu Brown

All rights reserved

To say thank you for purchasing this book, I offer you a free Video Course and more as a token of appreciation

Find the link to the Video Course at the end of this book.

Table of Contents

INTRODUCTION --5

Welcome to Trading. --5
    Importance of Financial Markets ---------------------------------------6
    What Will This Book Cover? ---7

CHAPTER ONE--13

Understanding Financial Markets. ---13
    What Are the Financial Markets? -------------------------------------13
    Types of Financial Markets. ---14
    Key Market Participants --16
    How Markets Operate. --18

CHAPTER TWO--23

The Basics of Forex Trading. --23
    Introduction to Forex Trading. --------------------------------------23
    Major Currency Pairs --24
    How Forex Trading Works. ---26
    Key Forex Terminology. ---27

CHAPTER THREE---33

Getting Started with Trading. ---33
    Choosing A Trading Platform ---------------------------------------33
    How to Open a trading account -----------------------------------35
    Understanding Leverage and Margin. ----------------------------37
    Set Up Your Trading Workspace ----------------------------------38

CHAPTER FOUR--43

Fundamental Analysis. ---43
   What is fundamental analysis? --43
   Key Economic Indicators ---44
   Analyzing Economic News --47
   How Fundamentals Influence Currency Prices -----------------------49

CHAPTER FIVE ---53

Technical Analysis. --53
   Introduction to Technical Analysis ------------------------------------53
   Reading Charts and Graphs ---54
   Key Technical Indicators ---56
   Identifying Trends and Patterns ---------------------------------------58

CHAPTER SIX --63

Create a Trading Strategy. ---63
   What is a trading strategy? --63
   Types of Trading Strategies ---64
   Developing a Trading Plan --66
   Back-testing Your Strategy --68

CHAPTER SEVEN --73

Risk Management. --73
   Importance of Risk Management ------------------------------------73
   Implementing Stop-Loss and Take-Profit Orders ----------------74
   Managing Trade Size --76
   Avoiding Common Pitfalls --77

CHAPTER EIGHT --83

Trading Psychology. --83
   The Role of Psychology in Trade -------------------------------------83
   Developing a Trading Mindset ---------------------------------------84
   Managing Stress and Emotions --------------------------------------86

Developing Confidence and Discipline. ------88

CHAPTER NINE------93

Practical Trading Tips. ------93
How to Analyze Market Trends------93
Tips for Successful Trading ------95
Avoiding Common Mistakes. ------97
Learn from Your Trades ------99

CONCLUSION------105

Trading for Beginners | *Chinedu Brown*

INTRODUCTION

Welcome to Trading.

Welcome to the fascinating world of trading! You've chosen a sensible choice whether you're looking to supplement your income, embark on a new profession, or simply pursue an interesting hobby. Trading can be an effective tool for attaining your financial objectives, but like any other skill, it requires knowledge, experience, and a smart approach.

In this book, we hope to demystify the trading process, with an emphasis on forex trading, which is one of the most popular and dynamic financial markets. As a newbie, you may feel overwhelmed by the sheer amount of information available and the sophisticated vocabulary that is frequently utilized. Our goal is to simplify these concepts and provide you with step-by-step guidance that will help you navigate the financial markets with confidence.

Importance of Financial Markets

The world economy depends on financial markets. They provide a marketplace for trading equities, bonds, currencies, and commodities. These markets help to allocate resources, control risk, and create wealth.

Forex trading, in particular, covers the trading of currencies, and it is the world's largest financial market, with daily trading volumes reaching $6 trillion. The forex market is open 24 hours a day, five days a week, providing several chances for traders worldwide. Understanding how this market works can provide you with significant insights into global economic trends and help you make sound trading decisions.

What Will This Book Cover?

This book serves as a detailed introduction for beginners. We will begin with the fundamentals, ensuring that you have a firm foundation before progressing to more complex topics. *Here's what you should expect to learn:*

Understanding Financial Markets: We'll look at several sorts of financial markets, their important participants, and how they operate. It will help you comprehend the larger setting in which forex trading takes place.

Basics of Forex Trading: It will help you learn what forex trading is, how it operates, and the essential terms. This part will provide the foundation for your trading journey.

Getting Started with Trading: We'll walk you through the process of selecting a trading platform, creating an account, and configuring your trading environment. This will prepare you for your initial trades.

Fundamental Analysis: This chapter will explain the notion of fundamental analysis, including how to evaluate economic data and news events that affect currency markets.

Technical Analysis: You'll learn how to read charts, apply technical indicators, and spot patterns and trends that can help you make trading decisions.

Creating a Trading Strategy: We'll help you develop a customized trading plan that includes strategies for both short-term and long-term trading.

Risk Management: Achieving success in the long run depends on adept risk management. We'll go over tactics for managing your trades and avoiding frequent errors.

Trading Psychology: Learning about the psychological components of trading will help you develop a resilient mentality, manage stress, and keep discipline.

Practical Trading Tips: We'll give you practical guidance and strategies for honing your trading skills and generating consistent profits.

Finally, we'll provide ideas for additional reading, tools, and groups to help you grow as a trader.

How To Use This Guide:

To get the most out of this book, approach it with an open mind and a desire to learn. Begin by learning the fundamentals and progressing to more complex topics. Each chapter is intended to build on the one before it; thus, sticking to the order is beneficial.

Do not hasten the process. Trading is a skill that develops over time. Practice what you've learned, and don't be disheartened by setbacks. They are part of the learning process. Keep a record of your trades and reflections to measure your progress and discover opportunities for growth.

Remember that trading is not about rapid success or quick profits. It's about laying a solid foundation, developing a systematic approach, and constantly honing your skills. With patience and dedication, you may navigate the financial markets with confidence and achieve your trading objectives.

Embrace the Journey

As you embark on this adventure, keep in mind that trading is as much about personal development as it is about financial gain. The abilities and discipline you develop along the way can help you with everything from decision-making to problem-solving.

We hope that this book will be a great resource for you on your trading journey, giving you the knowledge and tools you need to be successful. Approach each chapter with curiosity and excitement, remembering that every successful trader began out as a beginner.

Welcome to the world of trading. Your adventure starts today!

CHAPTER ONE

Understanding Financial Markets.

What Are the Financial Markets?

At their heart, financial markets are platforms where people purchase and sell assets such as stocks, bonds, and currencies. They serve an important role in the global economy, allowing firms to raise funds, investors to receive profits, and people to plan for their financial future. Consider financial markets to be a lively marketplace in which traders exchange financial products rather than fruits and vegetables.

The goal of these markets is to allocate resources efficiently. Companies issue stocks and bonds to raise funds for expansion, and investors buy and sell these assets to increase their wealth. Similarly, the forex market allows traders to speculate on currency movements, so global trade and investment patterns are altered.

Types of Financial Markets.

There are several major types of financial markets, each with a distinct function:

Stock markets: These are platforms for buying and selling shares of publicly traded corporations. Notable instances are the Nasdaq and the New York Stock Exchange (NYSE). Stock markets enable investors to own a piece of a company and provide corporations with access to capital.

Bond Markets: Bonds are debt securities issued by companies or governments. The bond market, which includes platforms such as the US Treasury market, enables companies to borrow money from investors and repay it with interest. Bonds are considered less risky than equities.

Commodity Markets: These markets deal with the trading of raw resources or primary agricultural goods such as oil, gold, and wheat. Commodity markets help to keep prices stable and provide chances to hedge against inflation.

Forex Markets: The foreign exchange (forex) market is the world's largest financial market. It involves currency trading and is open 24 hours a day, five days a week. Forex trading has an impact on everything from international travel expenses to global trade balances.

Derivatives Markets: Derivatives are financial contracts whose value is determined by the value of the underlying asset. These markets include options and futures contracts, which allow traders to speculate on price changes or hedge against risk.

Key Market Participants

Understanding who participates in financial markets helps us understand their dynamics.

Retail Traders: These are individual investors who trade for personal gain. Retail traders frequently use Internet platforms to make trades and invest in a variety of assets.

Institutional investors: Major financial institutions that handle substantial assets include pension funds, hedge funds, and mutual funds. Institutional investors frequently impact market patterns due to their huge transactions.

Market Makers: These companies provide liquidity by purchasing and selling assets at quoted prices. They help to ensure that there is always a market for buyers and sellers.

Brokers and Dealers: Brokers serve as go-betweens for buyers and sellers, whilst dealers trade securities for their own accounts. Both play critical roles in enabling transactions and maintaining market efficiency.

How Markets Operate.

Financial markets operate according to supply and demand concepts. Asset prices change depending on the buyer-seller balance. For example, if there are more buyers than sellers for a stock, the price will rise. Conversely, if more individuals want to sell, the price will drop.

Aside from supply and demand, economic data, geopolitical events, and investor attitudes all have an impact on markets. For example, a favorable jobs report can enhance stock values, whereas political unrest may generate market volatility.

When I initially began investigating financial markets, I was in my early twenties and eager to establish a name for myself in the trading world. My first experience was a mix of exhilaration and confusion. I remember enrolling in a stock market course only to be overwhelmed by the sheer amount of material. Terms like "market capitalization," "PE ratio," and "dividends" seemed strange.

One day, I decided to step back and simplify things. I visualized the stock market as a vast marketplace where businesses displayed their items (stocks) to potential purchasers (investors).

Prices fluctuated based on supply and demand, just as they would in a bazaar, and grasping this fundamental principle helped me navigate the complexity of trading.

I gradually came to recognize the nuances of each market type. I entered the forex market and learned that trading currencies were more than simply speculation; it was also about knowing global economic patterns and how they affect currency prices. This revelation changed my approach to trading, making it less about immediate gains and more about making informed decisions.

Understanding the financial markets is the first step in becoming a confident trader. Understanding the fundamentals of how markets work, the different types of markets available, and the roles of various participants can help you lay a solid foundation for your trading career. As you proceed through this book, you will expand on your understanding by delving into more particular parts of trading, such as forex and technical analysis.

Remember, financial markets are dynamic and complex, but with patience and continuous study, you can successfully navigate them. Accept the adventure, and allow your curiosity and perseverance to lead you to achievement.

Trading for Beginners | *Chinedu Brown*

CHAPTER TWO

The Basics of Forex Trading.

Introduction to Forex Trading.

Forex trading, which is also called foreign exchange trading, is the practice of buying and selling currencies to profit from market variations. The forex market is very accessible and liquid because it is open twenty-four hours a day, five days a week, unlike other financial markets. It is the biggest financial market in the world, with about $6 trillion worth of trading activity every day.

Forex trading is essentially about anticipating how one currency will move in relation to another. For example, if you feel the Euro would strengthen versus the US Dollar, you might consider buying EUR/USD. If the Euro's value rises, you can sell the pair for a profit.

Major Currency Pairs

The forex market trades in pairs of different currencies. There is a base currency and a quote currency in each pair. In a pair, the base currency comes first, then the bid currency. The price of the pair tells you how much of the stated currency you need to buy one unit of the base currency.

Here are some of the key currency pairs you'll come across:

- **EUR/USD (Euro/US Dollar):** Also known as the "Euro-Dollar" pair, this is the most traded currency pair worldwide. The US dollar is the quote currency, and the Euro is the base currency.

- **USD/JPY (US dollar to Japanese yen):** The base currency is the US dollar, while the quote currency is the Japanese yen.

- **GBP/USD (British Pound to US Dollar):** This combination, which often goes by the name as "Cable," denotes the British Pound as the base currency and the United States Dollar as the quoted currency.

- **USD/CHF (US Dollar to Swiss Franc):** The base currency, known as the "Swissie," is the US dollar, and the quote currency is the Swiss Franc.

How Forex Trading Works.

The speculation on currency pairing price changes is known as forex trading. Here's a simplified process of how forex trading works:

Choose a currency pair: Decide on the currencies you want to trade. For example, you might decide to trade EUR/USD.

Place an Order: Using your analysis, determine whether to purchase (go long) or sell (go short) the pair. Buying suggests you expect the base currency to rise versus the quote currency, whereas selling means you expect the base currency to fall.

Monitor Your Trade: After you place your order, keep an eye on the market to observe how the price of your preferred currency pair changes.

Close Your Trade: When you're ready to take your profit or cut your losses, close your trade by putting a sell order if you bought before and a buy order if you sold.

Key Forex Terminology.

Understanding the language used in forex trading is critical to understanding the market. Here are a few crucial terms:

Pips: These are the smallest units of price change in a currency pair. For the majority of couples, the value is 0.0001. For example, if EUR/USD goes from 1.1050 to 1.1051, it has moved one pip.

Lot: A lot is a pair of currencies' standard unit. The normal lot size is 100,000 units of base currency. There are mini lots (10,000 units) and micro lots (1,000 units).

Leverage: Leverage helps you to manage a huge position with a small quantity of capital. For instance, you can manage $100,000 worth of currency with just $1,000 if you have a 100:1 leverage.

Margin refers to the amount of money needed to initiate and sustain a leveraged position. It represents a percentage of the entire trade size.

I remember my first journey into forex trading. It was around ten years ago, and I was full of excitement and curiosity. I had recently started a trading account and was ready to make my mark on the forex market. I decided to trade the EUR/USD pair, which I had studied extensively about.

Initially, I put in a tiny purchase order, expecting the Euro to appreciate versus the dollar. I followed the trade intently, feeling both excited and nervous. The first several hours were nerve-racking since the price moved unexpectedly. I remember continuously checking my account, concerned about the slightest dip.

Fortunately, my analysis was correct, and the Euro began to appreciate. I opted to close the deal at a minor profit. The event taught me vital lessons about the emotional rollercoaster of trading, the value of remaining informed, and the need for a well-thought-out approach.

Becoming a profitable trader starts with understanding the basics of forex trading. Understanding how forex trading works, becoming acquainted with important currency pairs, and memorizing essential terminology will provide you with a firm basis for your trading adventure.

You'll build on these ideas and look into more sophisticated ideas and strategies as you read through this book. Recall that trading is an ongoing process of learning. All trades, whether profitable or not, help you develop as a trader. As you navigate the unpredictable world of forex trading, remember to remain engaged, disciplined, and most importantly, confident.

CHAPTER THREE

Getting Started with Trading.

Choosing A Trading Platform

As a new forex trader, one of the first things you'll need to do is pick a trading platform. You can make trades, keep an eye on the markets, and handle your trading account with a trading platform. It is your entry point to the forex market; thus, picking the appropriate one is critical.

When analyzing trading platforms, consider the following:

User Interface: The platform should be simple to use and navigate. Look for a clear, well-organized interface that fits your trading style and needs.

Features and Tools: Make sure the platform includes crucial tools such as real-time charting, technical indicators, and risk management capabilities. Advanced platforms may also incorporate automated trading features and configurable chart layouts.

Reliability: The platform must be stable and reliable, with little downtime. To evaluate the platform's performance, read user evaluations and use a demo account.

Costs and Fees: Some platforms charge commissions or spreads for trades, while others may impose monthly fees. Before making a commitment, ensure that you understand the cost structure.

Customer Service: If you have a technical problem or have inquiries, good customer service can come in handy. Look for solutions that provide responsive support across numerous channels.

How to Open a trading account

After you've decided on a trading platform, the following step is to open a trading account. *This process typically includes the following steps:*

Registration: Enter your personal information, including your name, address, and contact information. Some platforms may additionally request supplementary documentation for verification purposes.

Account Type: Select the type of account that best meets your trading needs. Most brokers provide a variety of account kinds, including normal, mini, and micro-accounts. Each category offers different minimum deposit amounts and leverage options.

Deposit funds: Fund your account using your favorite payment option. This could be done with a bank transfer, credit/debit card, or e-wallet. Make sure you understand the deposit and withdrawal procedures, as well as any applicable fees.

Verification: Complete any required verification steps to protect the security of your account. This could include giving identification documents or evidence of address.

Understanding Leverage and Margin.

Leverage and margin are key concepts in forex trading. They allow you to hold greater positions with less capital, but they also carry more risk.

Leverage: Leverage increases your trading ability. For example, using 100:1 leverage, you can control $100,000 in currency with only $1,000 of your own money. Leverage can boost your profits, but it can also increase your losses. Use leverage with caution, and be sure you completely grasp the repercussions.

Margin: Margin refers to the amount of money needed to initiate and sustain a leveraged position. It represents a percentage of the entire trade size. For example, if you are trading with 100:1 leverage, you will require a 1% margin. Be aware of the margin requirements for each currency pair and account type.

Set Up Your Trading Workspace

A well-organized trading area can boost your productivity and focus. Here's how to prepare your trading environment:

Choose a Reliable Computer: To avoid disruptions during trading, use a computer with a solid internet connection. Ensure that your system meets the technical criteria of your preferred trading platform.

Monitor Setup: Consider using numerous monitors to display charts, news feeds, and other important information at the same time. This setup can help you make more informed decisions and execute trades more efficiently.

Trading Software: Set up any additional software or tools you use for analysis, such as trading indicators, charting tools, or news aggregators.

Ensure that these tools work with your trading platform.

Comfort & Ergonomics: Design a pleasant and ergonomic workspace to reduce physical strain during extended trading sessions. To help with posture and prevent distractions, invest in a comfy chair and workstation.

Setting up my desk was a learning process for me when I first started trading. My initial setup was fairly simple: a single monitor and a laptop on my dining table. It worked, but it was not perfect. I regularly switched between different windows, which interrupted my concentration and hindered my decision-making.

Determined to increase my efficiency, I purchased a second monitor and set up a dedicated trading desk. I structured my charts and news feeds on distinct displays, allowing me to monitor numerous sources of information at once. This minor improvement greatly improved my trading experience. It showed me the importance of maintaining a well-organized workspace and how it may affect your overall performance.

Getting started with trading entails several critical steps, including selecting a reputable trading platform, opening a trading account, comprehending leverage and margin, and establishing an effective trading environment. By making informed judgments and attentively setting your environment, you may ensure a more enjoyable and effective trading experience.

Keep in mind that trading is a never-ending process of learning and adapting. Every action you take, from picking a platform to handling your trades, helps you grow as a trader. As you navigate the volatile world of forex trading, stay focused and organized, and constantly refine your approach.

Trading for Beginners | *Chinedu Brown*

CHAPTER FOUR

Fundamental Analysis.

What is fundamental analysis?

By considering relevant economic, financial, and qualitative elements, fundamental analysis is the approach used to determine the value of an asset. A key component of fundamental analysis for forex traders is the examination of economic indicators, geopolitical events, and central bank policies. The goal is to have a better understanding of the factors that could influence currency swings.

Fundamental currency analysis is to determine a currency's intrinsic worth using economic and financial information. This can help traders predict how currencies will fluctuate in response to changes in these fundamental causes. The primary difference between technical and fundamental analysis is that the former looks at broader economic trends and patterns, and the latter examines isolated price charts.

Key Economic Indicators

Forex traders might benefit from using economic indicators because they provide information about a country's economic health. Here are some of the most essential economic indicators to monitor:

Gross Domestic Product (GDP): GDP quantifies the total economic production of a nation. A rising GDP suggests an expanding economy, which can boost a currency. In contrast, a declining GDP might indicate economic troubles and devalue a currency. As a trader, monitor GDP figures to assess overall economic health.

Inflation Rate: Inflation is the rate at which prices for goods and services increase. Central banks frequently modify interest rates in reaction to inflation. Higher inflation usually results in higher interest rates, which might support the currency. However, if inflation is too excessive, it can erode purchasing power and reduce currency value.

Employment Data: Unemployment rates and nonfarm payrolls are two examples of employment indicators that provide insight into a nation's labor market. High employment typically indicates a robust economy, which can support a stronger currency. Rising unemployment, on the other hand, may imply economic difficulties and result in currency devaluation.

Interest Rates: Central banks use interest rates to manage monetary policy. Higher interest rates often attract foreign capital, which strengthens the currency. Lower interest rates can provide the opposite impact. Watch central bank meetings and remarks for signs about potential interest rate increases.

Trade balance: It refers to the difference between a country's exports and imports. A currency may appreciate in value if there is a trade surplus (more exports than imports), but it may weaken if there is a trade deficit (more imports than exports). This metric measures a country's economic competitiveness and trade linkages.

Analyzing Economic News

Economic news releases are scheduled events that provide useful information about current economic conditions. Key press releases include:

Economic Reports: GDP growth, inflation rates, and employment numbers are frequently given on a monthly or quarterly basis. These reports can cause substantial market moves, so keeping up with release dates is critical.

Central Bank Announcements: Central banks disseminate meeting minutes and statements on a regular basis. These pronouncements can provide insight into future monetary policy changes and influence currency values.

Geopolitical Events: Political events, international ties, and geopolitical developments all have the potential to influence currency markets. For example, trade negotiations, disputes, and elections can all cause market volatility.

To properly assess economic news, stick to credible financial news sources and use economic calendars to keep track of impending releases. Pay attention to market expectations against actual findings, as differences can cause dramatic currency changes.

How Fundamentals Influence Currency Prices

Fundamental factors affect currency prices by altering investors' expectations of economic stability and growth prospects. Here's how fundamentals affect currency values:

Economic Strength: A nation's currency may appreciate if it has a strong economy that draws in international investment. A currency's value can be supported by positive economic indicators such as strong GDP growth, low unemployment, and moderate inflation.

Monetary policy: Central banks have an important impact on currency valuation. Currency strength may be impacted by changes in interest rates and monetary policy. For example, raising interest rates can encourage capital inflows, thereby boosting the currency. In contrast, lowering interest rates might cause the currency to weaken.

Geopolitical Risks: Political instability or geopolitical tensions which can cause uncertainty and affect currency values. Currencies from countries undergoing political or economic crises may fall as investors seek safer assets.

When I initially started trading, my primary concentration was on technical analysis. I used charts and patterns to make trading decisions, but I quickly learned that understanding the larger economic context may help my strategy.

One noteworthy experience occurred during the global financial crisis. I was trading the Euro against the US dollar and observed extraordinary volatility. At first, I was perplexed since technical indicators did not adequately explain market trends. I decided to conduct a fundamental analysis, and I realized that the crisis was producing considerable changes in economic conditions and central bank policy.

By analyzing economic news and central bank statements, I developed a deeper knowledge of the fundamental causes that influence currency movements. This experience taught me the value of integrating fundamental analysis with technical strategies. It also demonstrated how economic and geopolitical issues can influence the forex market in ways that technical analysis alone may not detect.

Fundamental analysis is an effective method for determining the elements that influence currency fluctuations. Analyzing economic indicators, central bank policies and world events can provide helpful insights into market dynamics and help you make better trading choices.

As you progress through your trading adventure, include fundamental analysis into your strategy to improve your entire approach. Maintain awareness of global economic trends, monitor key indicators, and be responsive to changes in market conditions. With a strong understanding of fundamental analysis, you'll be better able to navigate the complexity of the forex market and reach your trading objectives.

CHAPTER FIVE

Technical Analysis.

Introduction to Technical Analysis

Technical analysis is a strategy for evaluating and forecasting the price movements of financial assets using past price data and trading volume. Unlike fundamental analysis, which examines economic indicators and market circumstances, technical analysis employs patterns and trends in price charts to forecast future price movements.

Many traders rely on technical analysis to better understand market activity and discover trading opportunities. It assumes that historical price patterns tend to repeat themselves and that prior trading activity may provide useful information about future price changes.

Reading Charts and Graphs

Charts are the primary instrument for technical analysis. They depict the historical price changes of an asset over time. The following are some common types of charts used in technical analysis:

Line Charts: Line charts are the most basic type of chart, showing merely the closing prices of an asset over a given period. They provide a good picture of the overall trend but lack specific information regarding price movements within the period.

Bar Charts: Bar charts provide more precise information, such as opening, high, low, and closing prices (OHLC) for each period. Each bar represents a certain time frame, such as an hour or a day, and depicts the range of price fluctuation over that period.

Candlestick Charts: Candlestick charts are popular in technical analysis because of their high visual detail. Each candlestick reflects OHLC prices over a specific time period. The candlestick's body depicts the opening and closing prices, while the wicks (or shadows) represent the high and low values. Candlestick patterns can provide information about market mood and future price reversals.

Key Technical Indicators

Technical indicators are mathematical calculations made using past price and volume data. They help traders recognize trends, momentum, volatility, and market strength. Some major technical indicators are:

Moving Averages (MA): To discover trends over a specific time frame, moving averages aggregate price data and smooth it out. Two of the most common kinds are the exponential moving average (EMA) and the simple moving average (SMA). Moving averages can help traders identify trend reversals, support and resistance levels, and more.

Relative Strength Index (RSI): The RSI calculates the pace and change of price movements to identify overbought or oversold positions. It spans from 0 to 100 and is commonly used to identify probable trend reversals. An RSI above 70 denotes an overbought condition, whilst an RSI below 30 indicates an oversold position.

Moving Average Convergence Divergence (MACD): An asset price's relationship between two moving averages is shown by the MACD, a momentum indicator that follows trends. The MACD, signal, and histogram lines make it up. The Moving Average Convergence/Divergence (MACD) is a tool that traders use to find likely buy or sell signals when moving averages converge or diverge.

Bollinger Bands: Bollinger Bands consist of a standard deviation-separated middle band (SMA) and two outer bands. They help traders identify volatility and probable price reversals. When the price is close to the top band, it may indicate overbought situations, whilst a price near the lower band may indicate oversold conditions.

Identifying Trends and Patterns

Technical analysis requires trend analysis as a fundamental component. Understanding market trends can help traders decide when to enter and quit trades. *Here are some frequent trends and patterns to watch for:*

Uptrend: An uptrend is defined by higher highs and higher lows. It signifies that buyers are in control and that prices are often rising. Traders search for purchasing chances in an uptrend.

Downtrend: When prices make lower highs and lows, it's considered a downtrend. It signals that sellers are dominating the market and that prices are falling. Traders may consider selling during a downtrend.

Sideways Trend: A sideways trend, also known as a range-bound market, happens when the price moves in a horizontal range without clearly moving up or down. In this case, traders frequently search for support and resistance levels to find prospective trading opportunities.

Common chart patterns include

Head and Shoulders: This pattern signals a reversal in the trend. A Head and Shoulders Top signals a negative reversal after an uptrend, whereas an Inverse Head and Shoulders signals a bullish reversal after a downtrend.

Double Top and Double Bottom: These patterns indicate potential trend reversals. A Double Top is a negative pattern formed after an uptrend, whereas a Double Bottom is a bullish pattern formed after a downtrend.

Flags and Pennants: As continuation patterns, flags and pennants show that the present trend will likely continue. lags are rectangular-shaped consolidations that occur after a large price move, whereas pennants are little symmetrical triangles that appear after a strong trend.

When i started trading, I was intimidated by the vast amount of data and indicators available. My first attempts at trading were focused purely on technical indicators, which frequently produced inconsistent outcomes. It wasn't until I really knew how to read and understand charts that I started seeing more consistent results.

One specific instance sticks out. I was trading the GBP/USD pair during a time of high volatility. Initially, I relied primarily on moving averages and RSI for my trades. However, I realized that my trades were not in line with market fluctuations. I decided to devote more time to researching candlestick patterns and chart formations.

I recall learning the Head and Shoulders design, which I initially found perplexing. However, after extensive practice, I noticed a Head and Shoulders Top pattern forming on the GBP/USD chart. Recognizing this pattern helped me foresee a bearish reversal, allowing me to change my trades accordingly. This event demonstrated the value of understanding both technical indicators and chart patterns.

Technical analysis is an effective tool for interpreting price trends and spotting trading opportunities. Mastering the use of charts, technical indicators, and trend patterns can help you improve your trading strategy and make better selections.

As you continue to develop your trading skills, combine technical skills with other strategies, such as fundamental skills, to create a more comprehensive approach. To navigate the forex market with confidence, practice consistently, remain up to date on market movements, and use your expertise in technical analysis.

CHAPTER SIX

Create a Trading Strategy.

What is a trading strategy?

A trading strategy is a methodical plan that directs your trading decisions and behaviors. It defines the criteria for entering and leaving trades, managing risk, and evaluating performance. Creating a trading strategy is important because it provides structure and discipline, allowing you to navigate the complexities of the financial markets.

A well-defined trading strategy allows you to be consistent and avoid emotional decisions, which can lead to bad trading results. It should be based on careful research and matched to your own trading style and goals.

Types of Trading Strategies

There are various trading strategies, each tailored to distinct market situations and trader preferences. Here are a few common types:

Trend Following: Finding the direction of the present market trend and trading accordingly is the essence of trend-following strategies. Traders employ indicators such as moving averages and trendlines to identify trends and enter trades that follow the trend's direction. A trader, for example, may purchase during an uptrend and sell during a decline.

Range Trading: Range trading entails determining support and resistance levels and trading within those limits. Traders purchase near support and sell near resistance, hoping to profit from price fluctuations within a specific range. Range trading is successful in markets with little or no trend.

Breakout Trading: When the prices break out of a particular range or pattern, breakout trading entails entering trades. Traders seek for breakout signals, such as increasing volume or momentum, and then enter trades in that direction. This strategy is designed to capture big price changes following the breakout.

Scalping: As a short-term trading strategy, scalping entails making numerous trades throughout the day in the hopes of profiting from slight price fluctuations. Scalpers rely on quick execution and tight spreads to maximize profits. This strategy necessitates strong focus and rapid decision-making.

Swing Trading: Swing trading is the practice of maintaining positions for several days or weeks in order to profit from medium-term price fluctuations. Traders employ technical analysis and market trends to determine entry and exit locations. Swing trading is ideal for those who enjoy a mix of short-term and long-term trading.

Developing a Trading Plan

A trading plan is a thorough document that details your trading strategy, goals, and rules. It serves as a road map for your trading activity, allowing you to stay disciplined. Here's how to develop a successful trading plan:

Define your goals: Begin by establishing clear and attainable trading goals. These could include explicit profit targets, risk management goals, or skill development milestones. Measurable and realistic goals are essential.

Select your trading style: Choose a trading strategy that corresponds to your personality, time availability, and risk tolerance. Whether you prefer day trading, swing trading, or long-term investing, your trading style should be consistent with your goals and lifestyle.

Create Entry and Exit Rules: Determine the criteria for entering and quitting trades. This could include technical indications, chart patterns, or fundamental factors. For example, you could enter a trade when a moving average crossing happens and exit when the price reaches a specific level.

Establish Risk Management Guidelines: Define how you will manage risk for each trade. This includes establishing stop-loss orders, calculating position sizes, and controlling leverage. Effective risk management protects your wealth while minimizing potential losses.

Establish a Record-Keeping System: Keep a trading notebook to log your trades, performance, and lessons learned. Recording your trades allows you to review and analyze your strategy, find strengths and shortcomings, and improve over time.

Back-testing Your Strategy

Back-testing is the process of testing your trading strategy against historical data to evaluate its efficacy. It allows you to evaluate how your strategy might have fared in the past and discover any difficulties before attempting to apply it to live trading. Here's how to back-test your strategy.

Gather Historical Data: Obtain historical price data for the assets you plan to trade by gathering historical data. This data should contain price, volume, and any other relevant factors. Trading platforms, data providers, and financial websites can all be used to get historical data.

Apply Your Strategy: Apply your trading strategy and simulate trades using historical data. Record the outcomes, including entrance and exit points, profit and loss, and overall performance.

Analyze Results: Evaluate your strategy's performance by looking at important indicators, including win rate, risk-reward ratio, and total profitability. Look for patterns or places for improvement, and make changes as necessary.

Refine Your Strategy: Based on your back-testing findings, revise your strategy to improve performance. This could include changing entrance and exit rules, tweaking risk management parameters, or adding new indications.

I had trouble developing a logical strategy. I frequently switched from one strategy to another, reacting to market noise rather than sticking to a planned plan. My outcomes were erratic, and I found myself making rash decisions that resulted in losses.

One watershed moment occurred when I decided to stand back and develop a formal trading plan. I began by setting concrete goals, such as making a 10% return on my trading capital in six months. I decided on a trend-following strategy based on moving averages and committed to applying it consistently.

To limit losses, I developed explicit entry and exit guidelines as well as a risk management plan. I kept a notebook of every trade, detailing my reasoning and results. Over time, I noticed a tremendous increase in my trading performance. The systematic method helped me maintain discipline and attention, resulting in more consistent outcomes.

This experience demonstrated the necessity of developing and adhering to a clear trading strategy. It taught me that successful trading involves a combination of planning, discipline, and ongoing evaluation.

A trading strategy is required for effective trading. You may enhance your trading performance and reach your goals by learning about various techniques, developing a comprehensive trading plan, and back-testing your approach.

As you construct your trading strategy, keep in mind that you must be versatile and willing to learn. The markets are dynamic, and your strategy should adapt to your experiences and changes in market conditions. With a sound strategy and disciplined execution, you'll be able to confidently navigate the financial markets.

CHAPTER SEVEN

Risk Management.

Importance of Risk Management

Risk management is a crucial component of trading that helps you to keep your trading capital safe. It entails locating, weighing, and ultimately removing any and all sources of risk. Even the most well-researched plans can lead to huge losses if they are not supported by a robust risk management plan. Effective risk management assists you in preserving capital, managing losses, and maintaining a long-term perspective on your trading operations.

Trading inherently entails unpredictability and volatility. Markets can be unexpected, and losses are a natural part of the trading process. Managing risk in a way that aligns with your trading goals and risk tolerance is the goal of risk management.

Implementing Stop-Loss and Take-Profit Orders

An essential part of risk management is using take-profit and stop-loss orders to limit your losses and keep your gains.

Stop-Loss Orders: A stop-loss order is intended to limit your losses on a trade by closing your position automatically when the price hits a predetermined threshold. Let's say you buy a pair of currencies at 1.2000 and set a stop loss at 1.1900. If the price falls below 1.1900, you will only lose 100 pip. This way, your position will be closed. Setting a suitable stop-loss level is determined by your trading strategy, market conditions, and the asset's volatility.

Take-Profit Orders: With a take-profit order, you can lock in your profits by having your position closed automatically when the price hits a certain level. For example, if you buy a currency pair at 1.2000 and set a take-profit level of 1.2200, your position will be closed when the price reaches 1.2200, resulting in a profit of 200 pips.

Setting a take-profit level allows you to capitalize on favorable price moves while avoiding the risk of a market reversal.

Managing Trade Size

Managing trade size, also known as position sizing, entails determining how much capital you should allocate to each trade. Proper position sizing helps you manage your risk exposure and avoid huge losses that could deplete your trading capital.

Here are some important factors for managing trade size.

Risk Per Trade: Establish a risk tolerance for each trade in relation to your trading capital. Every trade shouldn't risk more than 1% to 2% of your capital, as a general rule. For example, if you have a $10,000 trading account and elect to risk 1% on every trade, you will risk $100 on each trade.

Trade Distance: The distance between your entry point and stop-loss level influences your position size. If your stop-loss is 100 pips away from your entry and you're risking $100, you'll need to alter your position size to ensure that a 100-pip loss equals a $100 loss.

Leverage: You can control a larger share with less capital by using leverage. While leverage might boost profits, it also raises risk. Use leverage with caution and ensure that the size of your investment corresponds to your risk management plan.

Avoiding Common Pitfalls

Effective risk management necessitates an understanding of frequent dangers and proactive efforts to avoid them.

Overleveraging: Using excessive leverage can lead to significant losses, especially in volatile markets. Avoid the temptation to leverage too heavily and ensure that your leverage levels are appropriate for your risk tolerance.

Ignoring Stop-Losses: Failure to set or follow stop-loss orders might lead to higher losses than expected. Set stop-loss orders depending on your risk management plan and avoid moving them further away to avoid a loss.

Overtrading: Overtrading is when you take on too many trades or trade too frequently due to emotions or impatience. Overtrading can lead to greater transaction fees and increased risk. Stick to your trading plan and only trade when opportunities match your strategy.

Chasing Losses: Chasing losses entails taking on more risk or making hasty trades to recover losses rapidly. This behavior might lead to additional losses and emotional distress. Avoid making trades based on emotion and stick to your risk management trade plan.

One certain time, I rapidly realized the value of risk management the hard way. I was excited about a great trade setting and decided to go all in, expecting to double my capital in a short period of time. Unfortunately, the market did not move in my favor, and I incurred a substantial loss.

I understood that my lack of risk management had resulted in this circumstance. I had not set a stop-loss order, and I had committed too much capital to a single trade. This experience was a turning moment in my life. To preserve my capital and avoid making the same error, I understood I needed to develop a comprehensive risk management plan.

I started by establishing explicit risk limits for each trade and placing stop-loss and take-profit orders. I also began to monitor my trade size more carefully and avoided overleveraging. My trading performance gradually improved, and I felt more in control of my trades.

This experience taught me that risk management is more than a collection of rules; it is an essential component of trading that may have a substantial impact on your success. By implementing a disciplined risk management strategy, I was able to establish a more sustainable trading practice and produce better outcomes.

Risk management is a crucial component of trading in order to safeguard your capital, cut losses, and maintain a long-term perspective. Setting stop-loss and take-profit orders, regulating trade size, and avoiding frequent errors will help you navigate the financial markets with more confidence and discipline.

When developing your trading strategy, incorporate risk management techniques to protect your capital and improve your trading performance. Remember that effective trading needs not only a well-defined strategy but also an active approach to risk management.

Trading for Beginners | *Chinedu Brown*

CHAPTER EIGHT

Trading Psychology.

The Role of Psychology in Trade

Trading psychology encompasses the mental and emotional variables that influence your trading decisions. It has a significant impact on your success or failure as a trader. Understanding and regulating your psychological state can help you make better decisions, stick to your trading plan, and maintain discipline.

Trading can elicit a variety of feelings, such as fear, greed, and excitement. These emotions can impair your judgment and lead to rash judgments. For example, fear of losing money may force you to abandon a trade prematurely, whilst greed may motivate you to take unnecessary risks. Recognizing emotional triggers and learning how to handle them is critical to becoming a good trader.

Developing a Trading Mindset

Creating a trading mindset entails adopting attitudes and practices that promote effective trading. *Here are some crucial points to consider:*

- **Patience:** This is an essential trait for traders. Markets move at their own pace, and forcing trades or hurrying choices can lead to mistakes. Developing patience allows you to wait for good trading opportunities and avoid making rash judgments based on short-term market volatility.

- ***Discipline:*** This is the ability to stick to your trading plan and strategy on a consistent basis. It requires you to adhere to your entry and exit rules, maintain good risk management, and avoid emotional trading. Discipline allows you to remain focused and make judgments based on logic rather than emotion.

- **Adaptability:** Markets are dynamic and change quickly. Being adaptive helps you to modify your strategy and approach to changing market conditions. Flexibility in your trading approach enables you to respond to new knowledge and remain relevant in shifting situations.

- ***Confidence:*** This is essential for making sound decisions and taking sensible risks. However, overconfidence can be harmful.

It's critical to strike a balance between confidence and humility and to acknowledge that no strategy is perfect. Continuous learning and self-awareness aid in maintaining a healthy sense of confidence.

Managing Stress and Emotions

Trading can be stressful, particularly during moments of extreme volatility or when losses are incurred. Effective stress and emotion management is critical for retaining a clear mind and making informed judgments. *Here are some helpful strategies:*

- **Develop a Routine:** Establishing a daily trading routine adds structure and decreases stress. This practice could include chart analysis, evaluating your trading plan, and defining daily goals. A constant schedule allows you to remain organized and focused.

- ***Take Breaks:*** Taking regular breaks from trading can help you avoid burnout and refuel. Take a break from the screen, indulge in calming activities, and allow yourself time to unwind. Breaks help you maintain a balanced perspective and mitigate the effects of stress.

- ***Practice Mindfulness:*** Examples of mindfulness techniques that could help people unwind and concentrate better are deep breathing exercises and meditation. Mindfulness helps you stay present, reduce worry, and approach trading with a calm and balanced perspective.

- ***Stay Healthy:*** Mental and physical well-being are closely related. Get enough of sleep, exercise regularly, and eat a healthy, well-rounded diet. A healthy lifestyle allows you to make better decisions and manage stress more efficiently.

Developing Confidence and Discipline.

Building confidence and discipline involves consistent effort and self-reflection. Here are some tips for developing these traits:

Set Realistic Goals: Set goals that are within your trading plan and risk tolerance. Break down enormous goals into smaller, more attainable milestones. Achieving these milestones increases your confidence and reinforces good trading practices.

Review Your Performance: Regularly review and analyze your trading performance. Recognize your triumphs, identify areas for growth, and learn from your failures. This technique boosts confidence by highlighting accomplishments and providing opportunities for improvement.

Seek Feedback: Talk with other traders or mentors to get feedback and perspectives on your trading strategy. Constructive feedback allows you to improve your strategies, get fresh insights, and increase your confidence in your trading selections.

Celebrate Achievements: Recognize and appreciate your trading wins, no matter how modest. Celebrating achievements reinforces excellent behavior and encourages you to keep improving.

I had a bad experience with trading psychology in my early trading days. I was anxious for immediate profits and frequently let emotions guide my actions. After a series of impetuous trades and losses, I recognized how fear and greed were affecting my performance.

One critical event occurred when I made a hefty trade out of exhilaration following a string of winning trades. The trade did not proceed as intended, and I incurred a large loss. This experience led me to confront the emotional aspects of trading and their impact on my decisions.

Determined to overcome these obstacles, I began focusing on developing a disciplined trading routine and controlling my emotions. I incorporated mindfulness techniques into my everyday routine and made a concerted effort to be patient and stick to my trading plan. Gradually, my performance improved, and I felt more in control of my trading activity.

This experience taught me that trading psychology is as crucial as strategy and analysis. By addressing emotional triggers and developing a disciplined attitude, I was able to establish a more profitable and long-term trading practice.

Trading psychology is important to your success as a trader. You may increase your trading performance and reach your goals by understanding the impact of emotions, developing a positive mentality, and implementing stress and emotion management strategies.

As you develop in your trading career, continue to improve your psychological resilience and discipline. A balanced and attentive approach to trading allows you to make more informed judgments, maintain consistency, and confidently navigate the financial markets.

CHAPTER NINE

Practical Trading Tips.

How to Analyze Market Trends

Analyzing market trends is vital for making sound trading decisions. Trends indicate the general direction in which the market is moving and can help you spot prospective trading opportunities. Understanding how to interpret trends properly will help you make more profitable trades.

Identify the trend: Begin by determining the general direction of the market. Markets tend to move in three directions: uptrends, downtrends, and sideways trends. An uptrend is distinguished by higher highs and lower lows, whereas a downtrend has lower highs and lower lows. Sideways trends occur when the market moves in a range with no discernible direction.

Use Trend Indicators: You can use a variety of technical indicators to discover and analyze trends. Moving averages, such the Simple Moving Average (SMA) and Exponential Moving Average (EMA), smooth out price data while emphasizing trend direction. Trendlines and channels can also be used to visualize trends as well as potential levels of support and resistance.

Confirm with Volume: Volume analysis provides extra information about the strength of a trend. Increased volume during an uptrend or decline indicates that the trend is strong and likely to persist. Conversely, dropping volume during a trend may indicate a weaker trend or a possible reversal.

Tips for Successful Trading

Strategy, discipline, and constant development are all necessary for trading success. Here are some practical methods for increasing your trading success:

Create a Trading Plan: A well-defined trading plan outlines your strategy, goals, and risk-management guidelines. It serves as a road map for your trading activity and keeps you focused on your goals. Your plan should include criteria for entering and leaving trades, as well as risk management rules.

Stay Informed: Stay current on market news, economic events, and geopolitical happenings that may affect the financial markets. Staying educated allows you to predict market moves and make smart trading decisions. Subscribe to financial news sources and use economic calendars to keep track of major events.

Maintain a Trading Diary: You can record your trades, evaluate your performance, and draw lessons from your trades by keeping a trading diary. Keep track of trade setups, entry and exit points, reasoning for the trade, and results. Reviewing your journal allows you to find patterns, refine your strategy, and avoid repeating mistakes.

Continuously Learn and Adapt: The financial markets are continuously changing, and effective traders must remain adaptive and open to new ideas. Invest in your education by reading trading books, attending webinars, and joining trading forums. Adapt your strategies to fresh insights and changing market conditions.

Avoiding Common Mistakes.

Avoiding frequent trading mistakes is critical to long-term success. *Here are some hazards to look out for:*

- ***Overtrading:*** Overtrading occurs when you take on too many trades or trade too frequently. This conduct can lead to higher transaction costs, increased risk exposure, and mental discomfort. Follow your trading plan and trade based on valid signals rather than making rash selections.
- ***Ignoring Risk Management:*** Neglecting risk management can lead to significant losses and jeopardize your trading capital. Always utilize stop-loss orders, limit your trade size, and follow your risk management guidelines. Long-term success depends on protecting your capital.

- ***Chasing Losses:*** Chasing Losses is the practice of making hasty trades in order to swiftly recover earlier losses. This activity can lead to additional losses and exacerbate emotional distress. Avoid making trades based on emotional reactions, and stick to your trading plan.

- ***Failure to Adapt:*** Markets evolve with time, and strategies that worked in the past may not be effective in the current environment. Maintain your flexibility and willingness to alter your approach in response to fresh knowledge and changing market factors.

Learn from Your Trades

Learning from your experiences is one of the most important components of trading. Analyzing your trades and understanding what worked and didn't will help you fine-tune your strategy and boost your performance. *Here's how to get the most out of your trading experiences.*

Review Your Trades: Conduct regular reviews of your trades to determine their efficacy and find areas for improvement. Analyze both successful and unsuccessful trades to identify the elements that influenced their outcomes.

Identify Patterns: Look for patterns in your trading habits, such as repeating blunders or effective strategies. Identifying these patterns might help you make better decisions and change your strategy accordingly.

Seek Feedback: Talk to other traders or mentors to get feedback and perspectives on your trading techniques. Constructive feedback might help you get vital insights and improve your trading skills.

Celebrate Successes: Recognize and appreciate your trading wins, no matter how modest.

Celebrating achievements reinforces excellent behavior and encourages you to keep improving.

Early in my trading career, I faced a number of hurdles that taught me vital trading lessons. One notable experience was a series of trades in which I tried to recoup losses by taking on increasingly huge stakes. My intention was to repay prior losses rapidly; however, this method resulted in even higher losses and severe frustration.

It marked a turning point for me. I discovered that my fixation on recovering losses was clouding my judgment and driving me to depart from my trading plan. I stepped back, reevaluated my strategy, and put in place tougher risk management guidelines. By focusing on disciplined trading and learning from my failures, I was able to improve my performance and obtain more consistent outcomes.

This experience showed me the value of not making rash judgments and sticking to a well-defined trading plan. It also highlighted the importance of ongoing learning and self-reflection in honing my trading abilities.

Practical trading strategies, such as evaluating market trends, avoiding frequent mistakes, and learning from trades, are critical for success in trading. By following these recommendations and implementing the lessons you've learned from your experiences, you may improve your trading performance and navigate the financial markets more confidently.

Stay disciplined, informed, and devoted to your trading plan as you progress through your trading career. Accept the learning process and see each trade as an opportunity to improve and develop your approach. You may reach your trading goals and establish a successful trading practice if you are persistent and dedicated.

Trading for Beginners | *Chinedu Brown*

CONCLUSION

When you finish this guide, it's important to reflect on the journey you've traveled and the foundation you've established. Trading is a talent that involves ongoing study, practice, and adaptability. The knowledge and strategies described in this book are intended to help you navigate the complexity of the financial markets with confidence. This final chapter tries to highlight essential topics, detail the next steps in your trading adventure, and offer some final words of encouragement.

Summary of Key Concepts

Throughout this book, we've covered a wide range of topics to provide you with a basic understanding of trading fundamentals.

Introduction to Trading: We started by looking at the fundamentals of trading, understanding the importance of financial markets, and learning how to use this guide efficiently. You should now have a thorough understanding of what trading entails and how financial markets work.

Understanding Financial Markets: We looked at the nature of financial markets, the various types of markets, essential participants, and how they work. This understanding provides context for making intelligent trading decisions and comprehending market dynamics.

Basics of Forex Trading: We introduced you to forex trading by describing main currency pairings, how they work, and key terms. This fundamental understanding is required for anyone wishing to trade in the foreign exchange market.

Getting Started with Trading: Choosing a Trading Platform, opening a Trading Account, Understanding Leverage and Margin, and Setting Up Your Trading Workspace were all topics covered in the trading course. These practical procedures are critical for establishing and preparing your trading business.

Fundamental Analysis: We studied fundamental analysis ideas such as major economic indicators and news analysis and understood how fundamentals affect currency markets. This research allows you to make more informed trading selections based on economic and financial data.

Technical Analysis: We looked at approaches for reading charts and graphs, using key technical indicators, and detecting trends and patterns. Technical analysis is essential for understanding price movements and making informed trading decisions.

Building a Trading Strategy: We talked about the necessity of having a trading strategy, the many types of strategies, building a trading plan, and back-testing your strategy. A well-defined strategy allows you to approach trading systematically and with purpose.

We stressed the necessity of risk management, which includes placing stop-loss and take-profit orders, controlling trade size, and avoiding frequent errors. The preservation of your trading capital and the attainment of sustained success depend on your ability to employ effective risk management strategies.

Trading Psychology: We investigated the role of psychology in trading, such as developing a trading mindset, dealing with stress and emotions, and increasing confidence and discipline. Understanding trading psychology allows you to remain focused and make sensible decisions.

Practical Trading Tips: We provided practical advice on evaluating market trends, avoiding frequent blunders, and learning from your trades. These ideas are intended to help you improve your trading skills and performance.

Finally, we looked into several resources for ongoing learning, such as recommended books, courses, websites, tools, and trading groups. Continuous learning and keeping up with market news are critical for continued improvement.

Next Steps in Your Trading Journey

With the underlying knowledge and practical suggestions presented in this book, you are now prepared to begin your trading journey. Here are some actions to help you move forward:

Implement your trading plan: Begin by putting your prepared trading plan into action. Apply the strategies and approaches you've studied to actual trading settings. Begin with a demo account if necessary to practice without risking real money.

Monitor and Adjust: Review your trading performance on a regular basis and make any necessary adjustments to your strategies. Analyze your trades, monitor your progress, and make any required changes to improve your strategy.

Stay Informed: Stay current on market news, economic trends, and changes in trading laws.

Staying informed will allow you to adjust to market situations and make informed judgments.

Engage with the Trading Community: Meet other traders, join trading forums, and engage in debates. Participating in the trading community provides essential insights, support, and possibilities for growth.

Continue Your Education: Invest in your education by reading advanced trading books, taking more classes, and attending seminars. Continuous learning is vital for honing your abilities and keeping competitive in the trading industry.

Embracing Continuous Improvement

Trading is a never-ending learning experience. As you gain more experience and knowledge, enjoy the learning process and be open to new ideas and strategies. Here are several approaches to promoting continuous improvement:

Seek input: Regularly solicit input from mentors, peers, or trading groups. Constructive feedback can help you get useful insights and discover areas for improvement.

Experiment with New Strategies: Do not be scared to try new trading strategies and tactics. Testing multiple tactics can help you figure out what works best for you and improve your trading strategy.

Reflect on Your Progress: Take time to consider your progress and accomplishments. Recognize your success and learn from any failures. You stay motivated and goal-focused when you reflect on your goals.

As you reach your initial trading goals, set new ones to push yourself and progress. Setting specific and attainable goals helps you stay motivated and driven.

Final Words of Encouragement.

Trading is both an art and a science that requires dedication, patience, and perseverance. As you begin your trading career, realize that success does not happen immediately. It takes time, effort, and a will to learn from both achievements and failures.

Believe in yourself, keep disciplined, and maintain a positive attitude. Trading might be difficult, but with the correct knowledge, tools, and attitude, To accomplish your trading goals, you can effectively navigate the financial markets.

We appreciate you taking the time to read this information. I wish you the best of luck on your trading journey and hope that you achieve success and fulfillment. Keep in mind that every trade offers the chance to learn and develop, so relish the experience and never give up on your dreams of excellence.

GET INSTANT ACCESS TO THE FREE VIDEO COURSE BY CLICKING OR COPYING AND PASTING THE LINK BELOW TO YOUR BROWSER!!

https://mailchi.mp/8465a286d83d/chinedu-brown-fx

Happy Watching!!